Bedtime Blessings

Photographed and hand painted by Kathleen Francour

Stories by Sylvia Seymour

Photography © 2002 Kathleen Francour
Carefree, Arizona. All rights reserved.

Copyright © 2002 Publications International, Ltd.
All rights reserved. This publication may not be reproduced or quoted
in whole or in part by any means whatsoever without written permission from

Louis Weber, C.E.O.
Publications International, Ltd.
7373 North Cicero Avenue
Lincolnwood, Illinois 60712

www.pubint.com

Permission is never granted for commercial purposes.
Jesus Loves the Little Children is a trademark of Publications International, Ltd.
Manufactured in China.

ISBN: 0-7853-7047-1

A Monster in My Closet

"There's a monster in my room!" David peeked out from under the covers. His heart was pounding. "Grrrrr!" roared the monster.

The monster was in his closet! David pulled the covers higher over his head. "Grrrrr!" roared the monster again. What should David do?

"Dear Jesus, Mommy says that You are always with me. Please help me not to be afraid." David slipped out from under the covers. He was trembling, but he knew that Jesus would protect him. He opened the closet door slowly.

"Grrrrrr," growled his little puppy shaking an old shoe in his mouth. "Grrrrr."

"Oh, Baxter," David laughed, "it's just you."

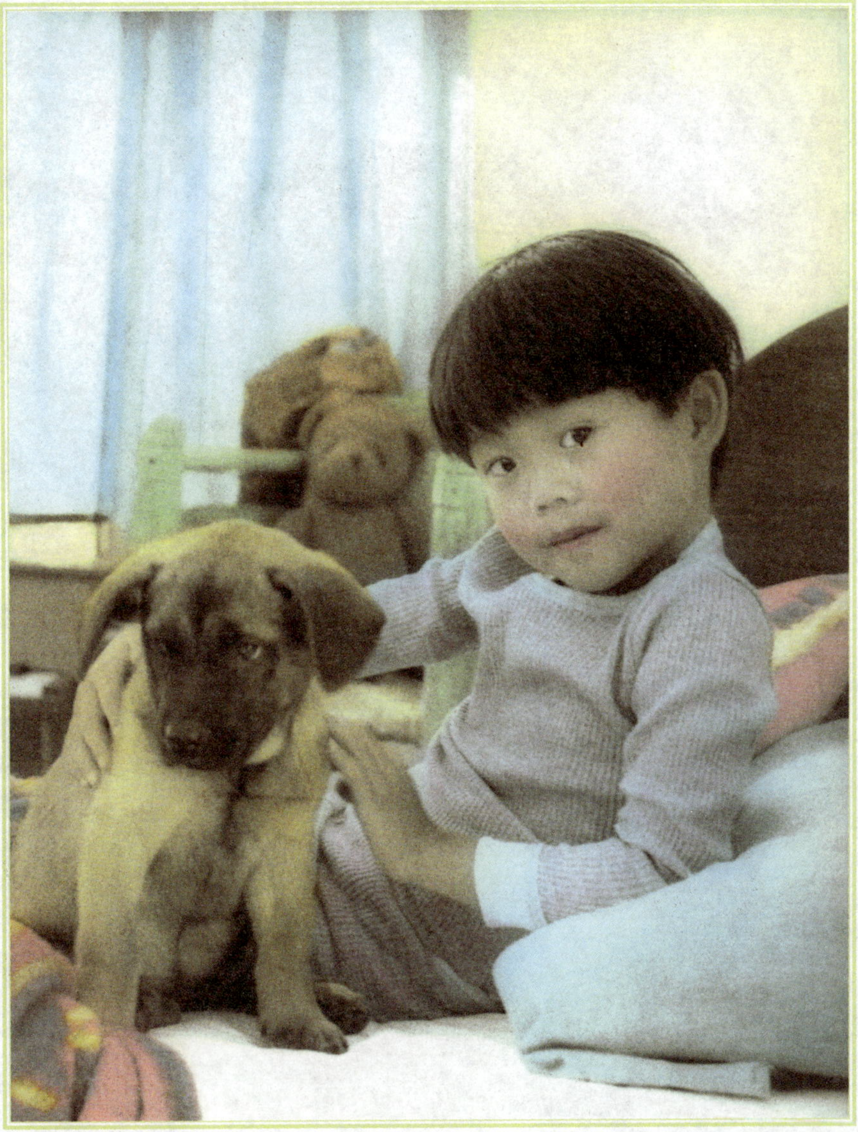

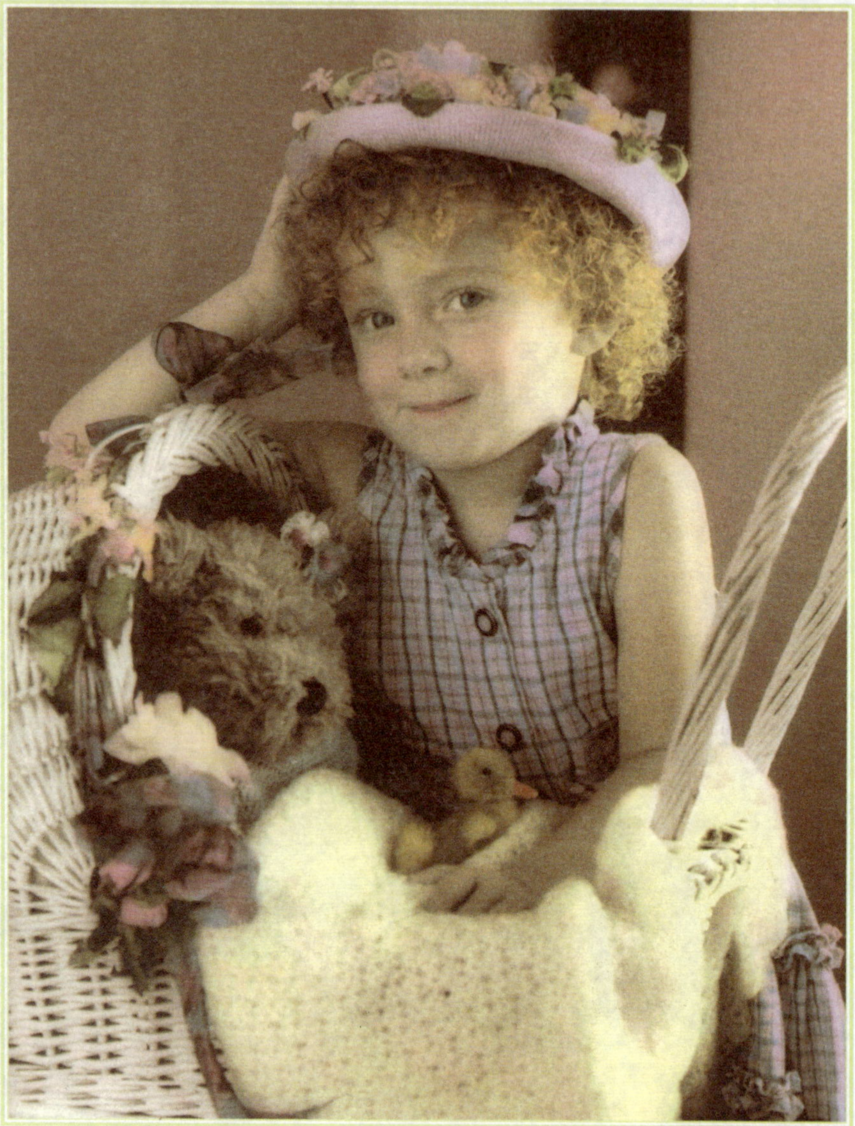

Now I lay me down to sleep.
    I pray Thee, Lord, my soul to keep.
Your love be with me through the night
    And wake me with the morning light.

Lord, keep us safe this night,
    Secure from all our fears.
May angels guard us while we sleep,
    Till morning light appears.

In my little bed I lie,
   God, my Father, hear my cry;
Please protect me through the night,
   Keep me safe till morning light.
Amen.

Bye, baby bunting,
   Thy father's gone a-hunting.
He's gone to catch a moonbeam bright
   To guard you as you sleep tonight.

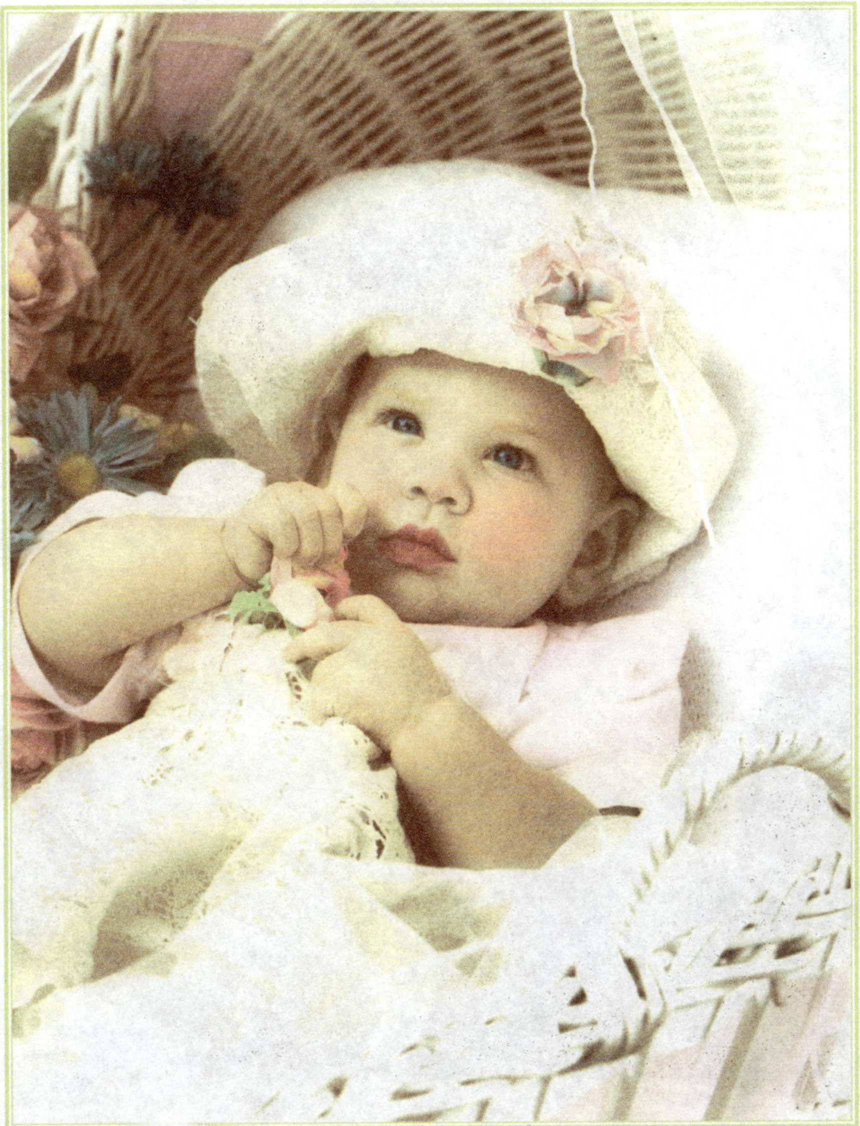

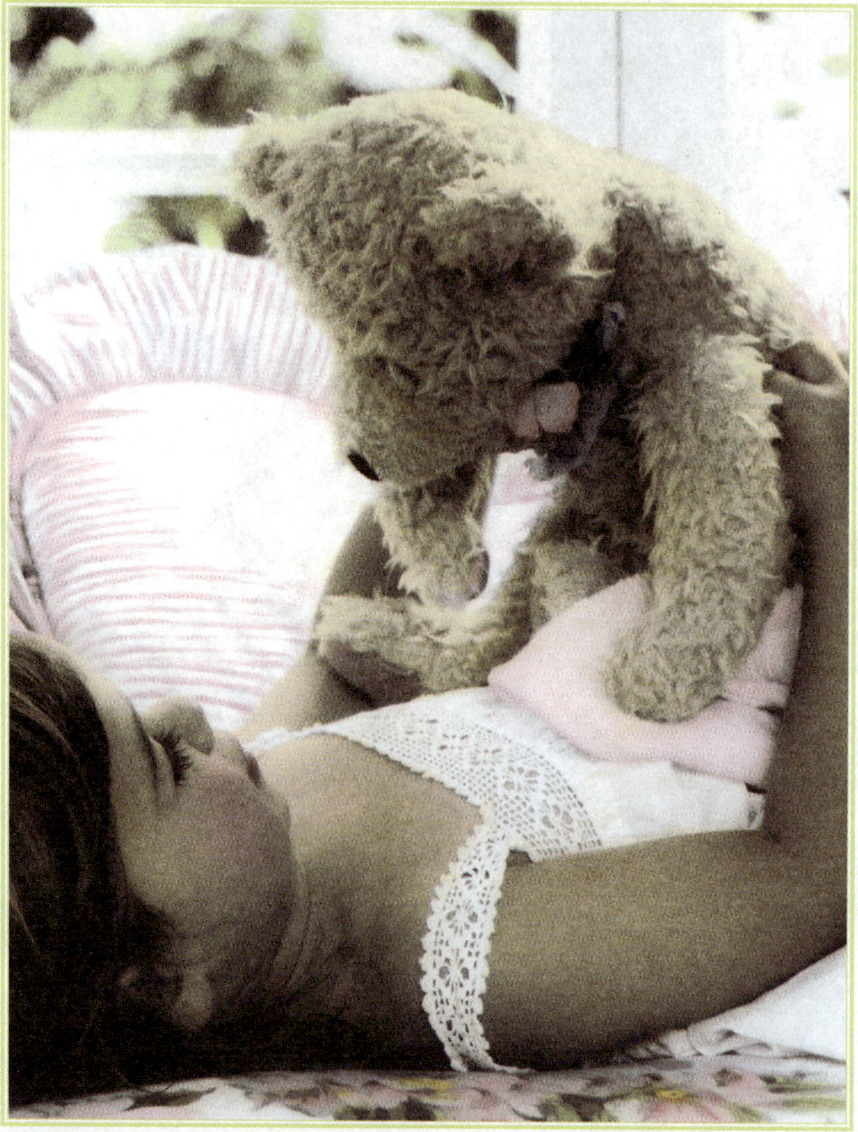

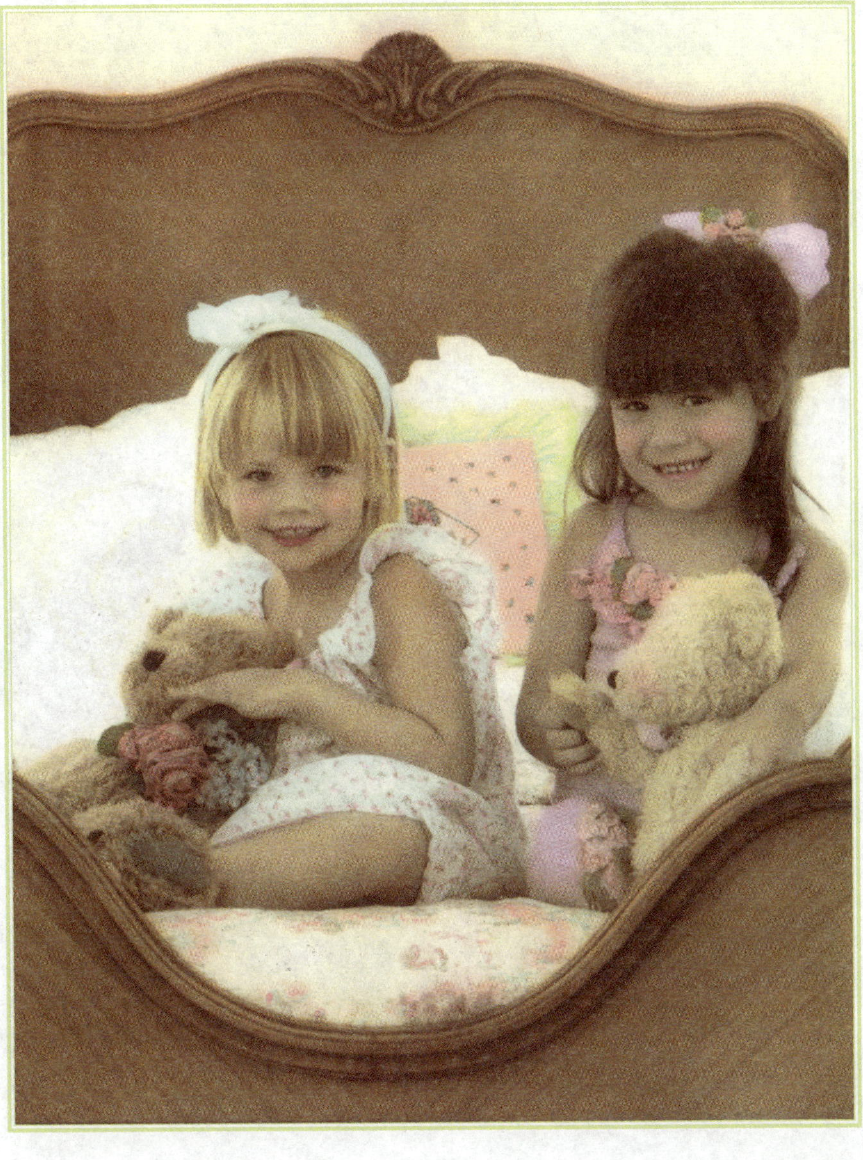

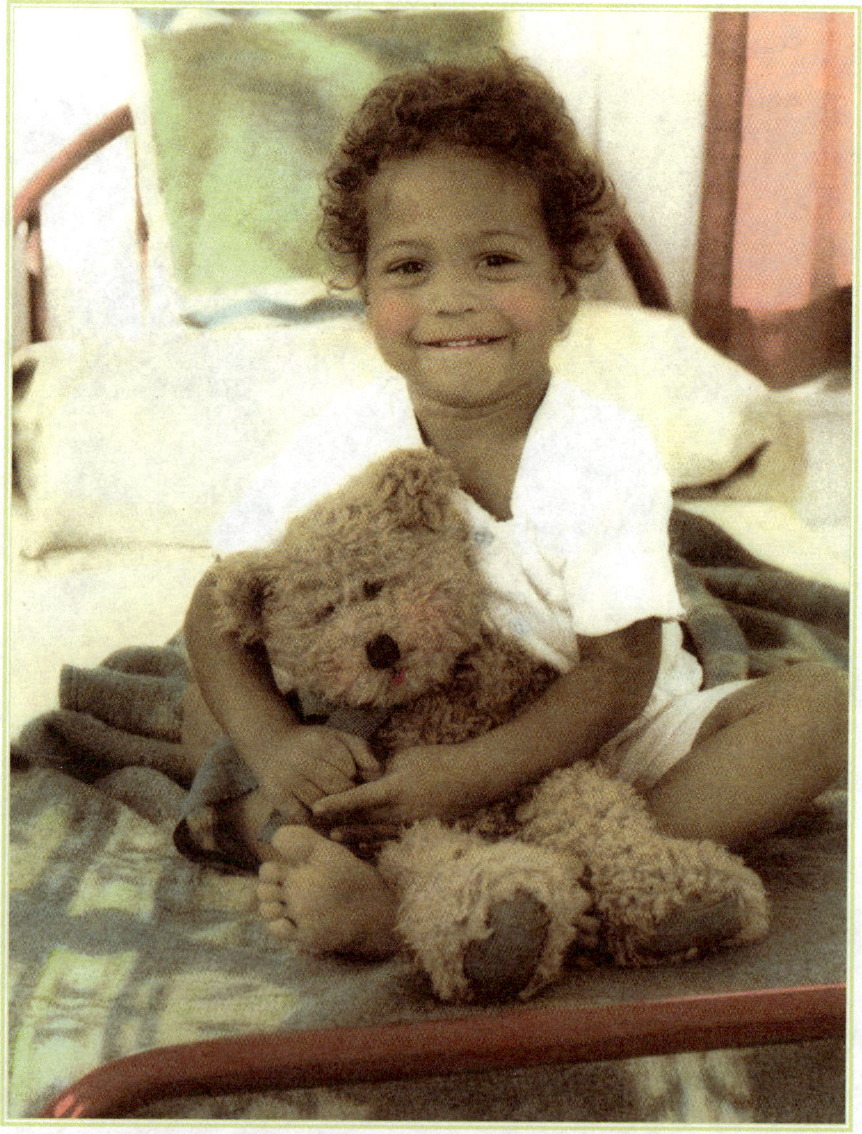

Father, bless me in my body.
    Father, bless me in my soul.
Father, bless me this night
    In my body and my soul.

Jesus said:

"Do not worry about tomorrow,
for tomorrow will worry about itself. Each
day has enough trouble of its own."

Matthew 6:34

Sleep, my child, and peace attend thee,
    All through the night;
Guardian angels God will send thee,
    All through the night,

Soft and drowsy hours are creeping,
    Hill and vale in slumber sleeping,
I my loving vigil keeping,
    All through the night.

While the moon her watch is keeping,
    All through the night,
While the weary world is sleeping,
    All through the night,

O'er thy spirit gently stealing,
    Visions of delight revealing,
Breathes a pure and holy feeling,
    All through the night.

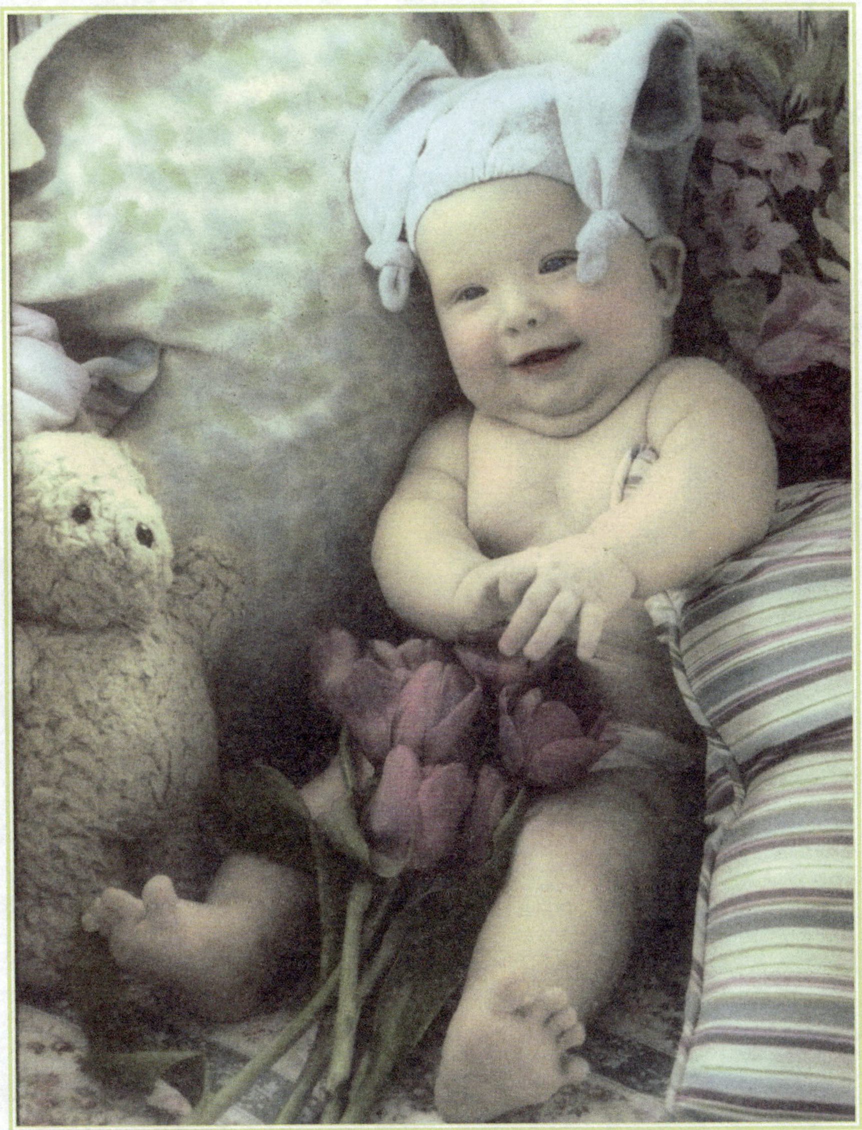

Good night! Good night!
Far flies the light;
But still God's love
Shall flame above,
Making all bright.
Good night! Good night!

Victor Hugo

Sleep Well

"It's time for bed, Casey," said Mother as she came into the bedroom to tuck in her daughter.

"Mommy, does Jesus really listen to my prayers?"

Mother looked at Casey's trusting face. "Yes, Casey, Jesus loves you and wants you to talk to Him."

"I'm sure other kids talk to Him, too. Maybe He's too busy to listen," said Casey.

"Jesus always has time to listen to a child's prayer."

Casey began to pray, "Dear Jesus, I love You. Thank you for Mommy and Daddy. Thank you for my house. Thank you for letting me play. Bless Teddy and help him not to be afraid in the dark."

I will lie down and sleep in peace, for You alone, O Lord, make me dwell in safety.

Psalm 4:8

Be near me, Lord Jesus; I ask Thee to stay
    Close by me forever, and love me, I pray;
Bless all the dear children in Thy tender care,
    And fit us for heaven to live with Thee there.

Lord Jesus,
Sometimes at night I am scared.
I think I hear noises and see strange shadows.
Lord, help me to remember that You are with me
And that I need not be afraid.

Amen.

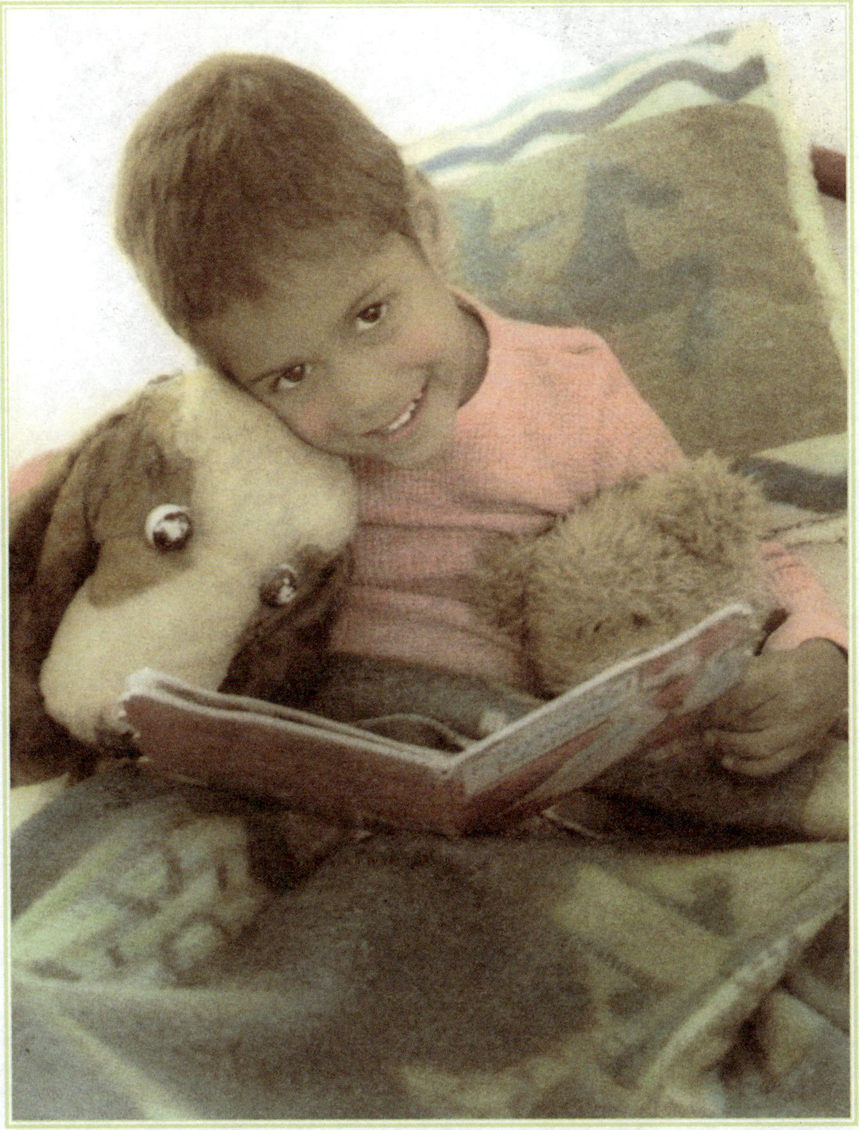

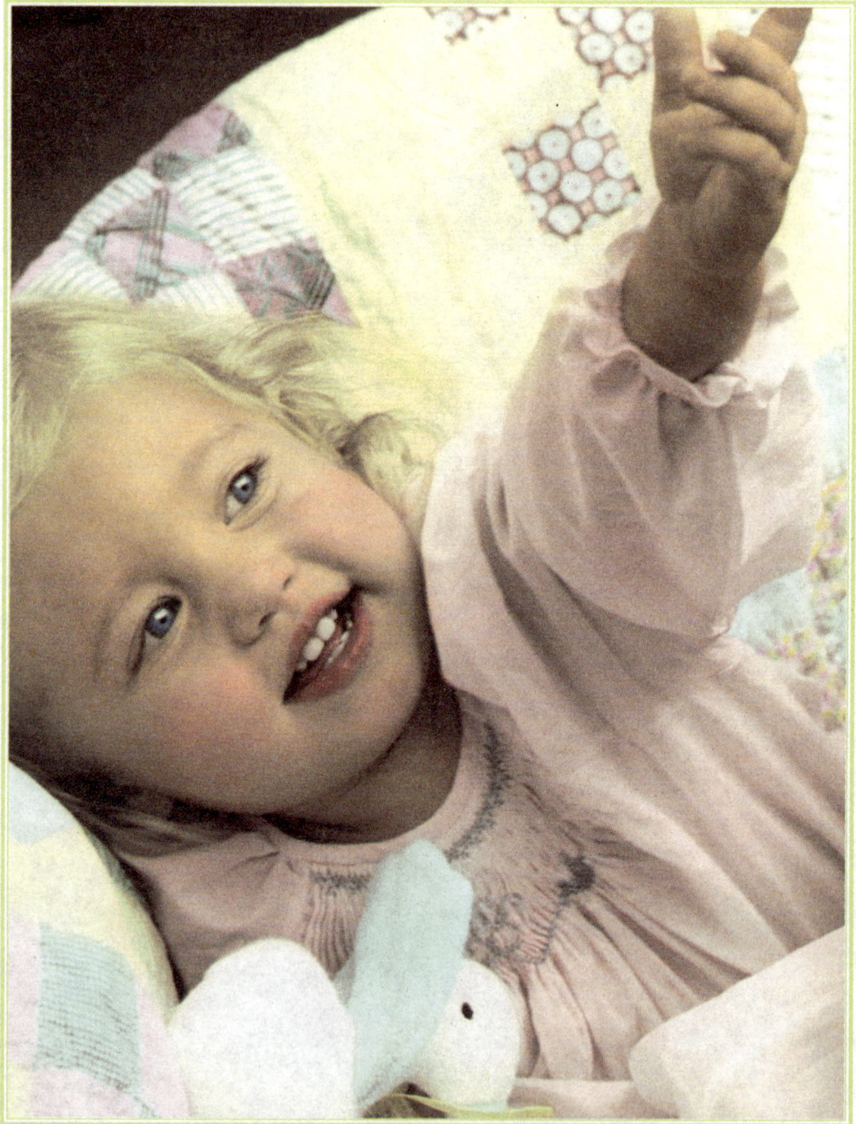

I see the moon.
The moon sees me.
God bless the moon,
And God bless me.

The moon shines bright,
The stars give light
Before the break of day;
God bless you all,
Both great and small,
And send a joyful day.

Who Can Count the Stars?

Mary and Catherine sat beside the window. It was time for bed, but Mother said they could say good night to the moon and stars.

"Good night, moon and all the stars," said Mary as she looked out at the night sky.

"I can count the stars," Catherine bragged. "Two, three, four, fifteen, sixteen,…"

"No Catherine," Mary interrupted. "No one can count all the stars!"

"No one?"

"No one," Mary paused. "No one but God. God knows all the stars. God is so wonderful that He calls each star by name."

Good Morning, God

Photographed and hand painted by Kathleen Francour
Stories by Sylvia Seymour

Photography © 2002 Kathleen Francour
Carefree, Arizona. All rights reserved.

Copyright © 2002 Publications International, Ltd.
All rights reserved. This publication may not be reproduced or quoted
in whole or in part by any means whatsoever without written permission from

Louis Weber, C.E.O.
Publications International, Ltd.
7373 North Cicero Avenue
Lincolnwood, Illinois 60712

www.pubint.com

Permission is never granted for commercial purposes.
Jesus Loves the Little Children is a trademark of Publications International, Ltd.
Manufactured in China.

ISBN: 0-7853-7051-X

Jesus Loves the Little Children

Rise and Shine

Lucy did not want to get up. It was too early. Why couldn't she sleep a little longer? She dragged herself out of bed and stood looking out of her window. The sun was like a tiny face peeking over the tree tops.

"Hello, sun," Lucy said yawning. "Do you hate to wake up, too?"

The sun was bigger now, spreading its light across the sky like a gentle smile.

"Lucy," Mother called, "breakfast is ready."

She stretched sleepily and thought about the tasty breakfast waiting for her downstairs. She smiled at the happy sun and whispered, "Thank you, Jesus, for the morning sun. And thank you for this new day."

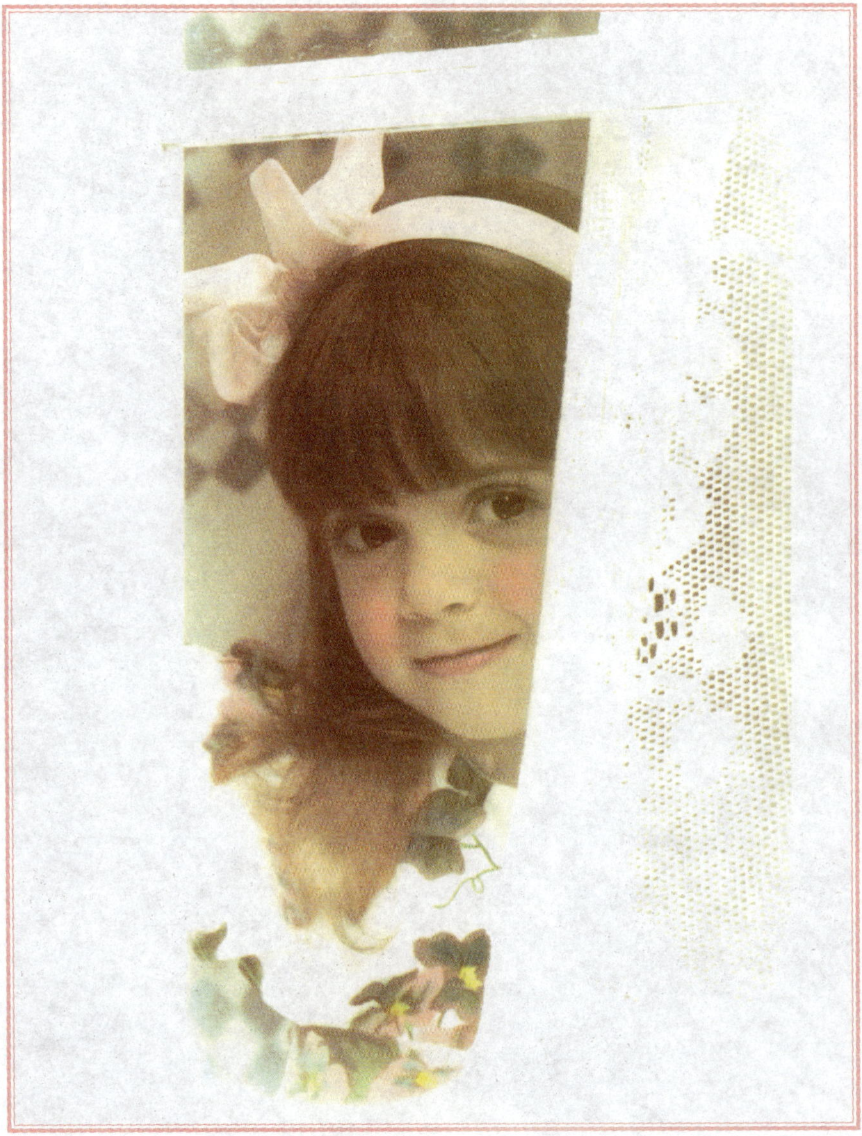

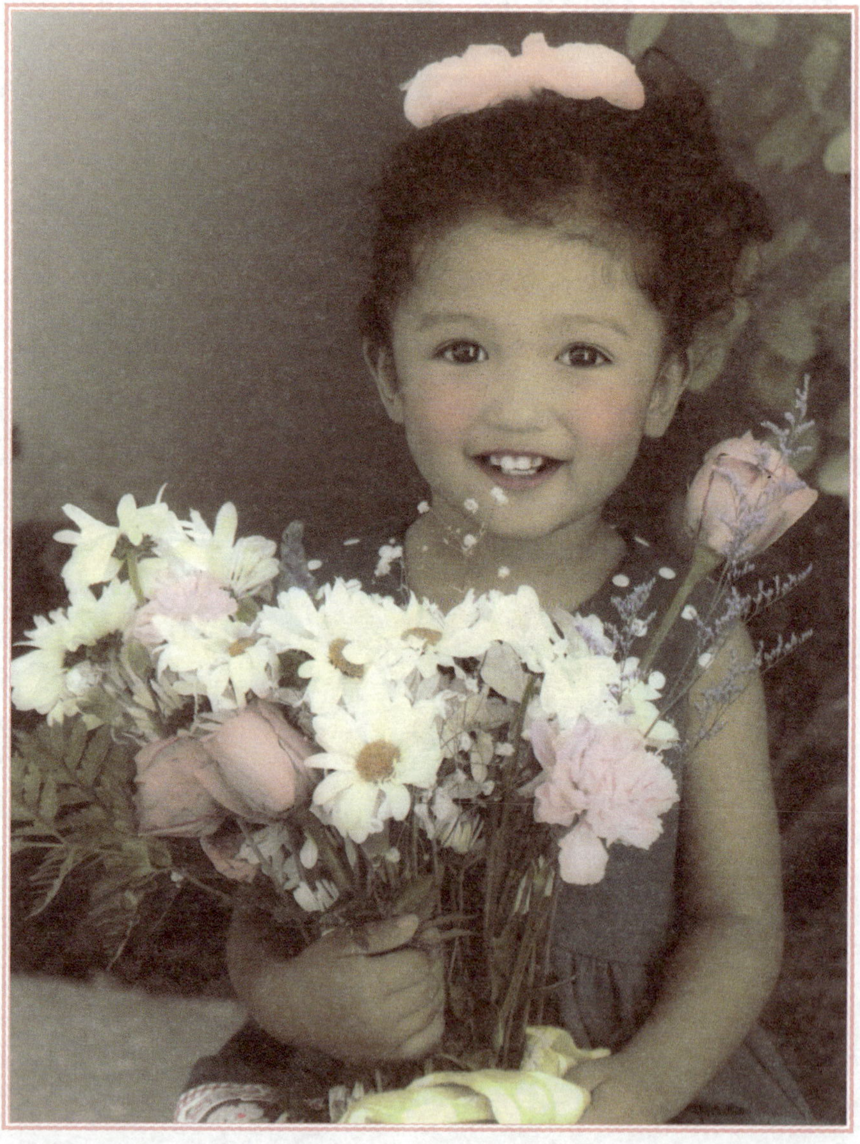

I am small,
my heart is clean;
let no one dwell in it
except God alone.

This morning, God,
this is Your day.
I am Your child.
Show me Your way.
      Amen.

Lord Jesus Christ, be with me today,
    And help me in all I think, and do, and say.

O God, Creator of Light,
At the rising of Your sun this morning,
let the greatest of all light, Your love,
rise like the sun within our hearts.
                    Amen.

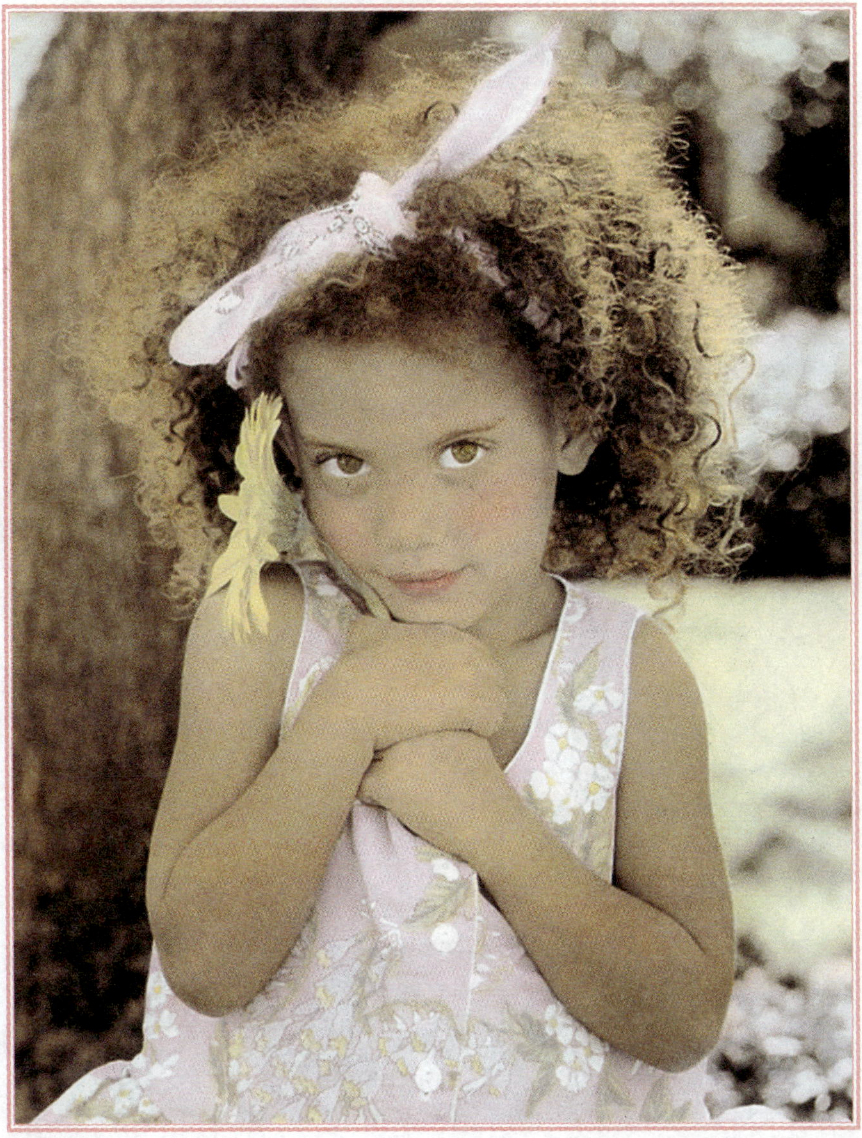

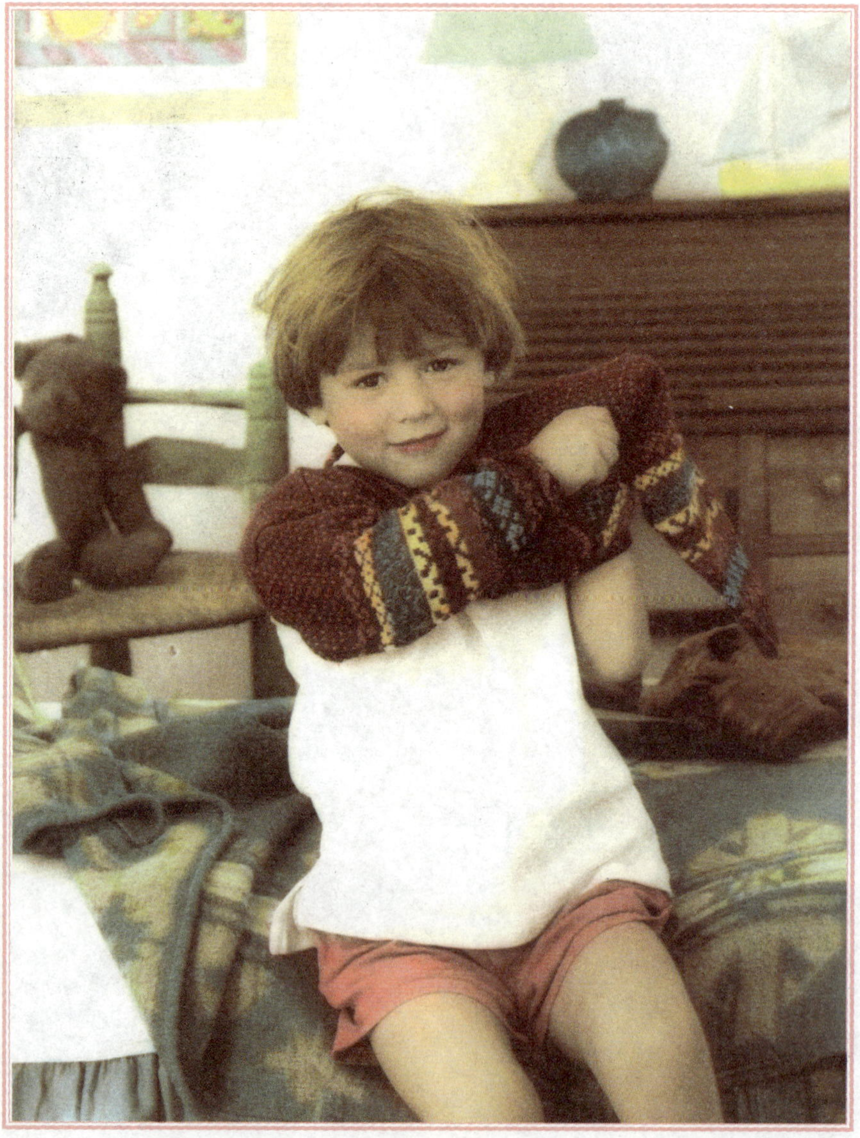

A Surprise for Mommy

"I'll surprise Mommy this morning!" Johnny whispered happily. "I'm a big boy and I can get dressed by myself." He wiggled his head and arms through his pullover shirt and stepped into his shorts. They were a little bit crooked, but the tag was in the back like Mom said.

Johnny pulled on his socks. "Now, which shoe?" he thought. "Jesus will help me. He always helps me when I ask Him." Johnny closed his eyes and prayed. "Dear Jesus, please help me find the right shoe." He put his foot into his shoe. It fit! The other shoe was a perfect fit, too.

"Look Mommy," called Johnny. "I did it! I did it!"

Good morning, Lord!
Be with me all day long,
until the shadows lengthen,
and the evening comes,
and the hustle and bustle of life is done,
and those at work are back at home.
Then in Thy mercy, grant us safe lodging,
and a Holy rest, and peace at the last.
                                        Amen.

Lord, teach us to pray.

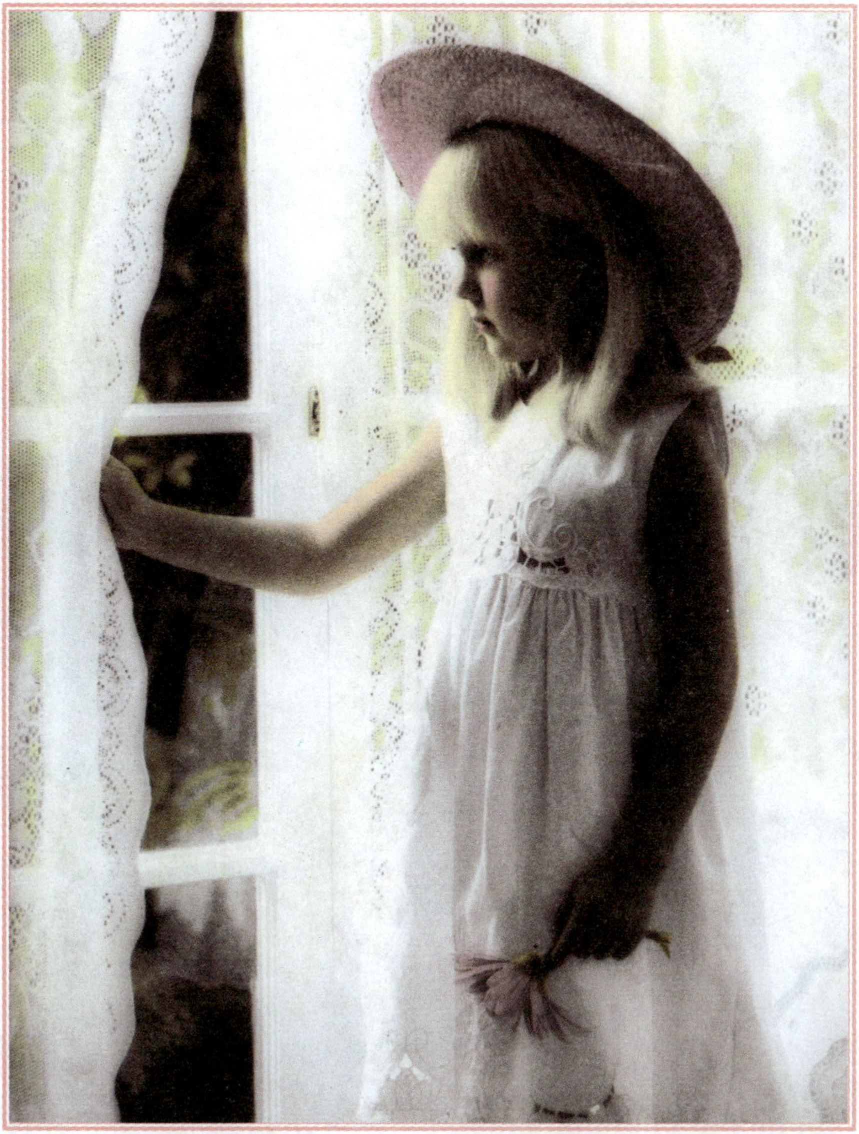

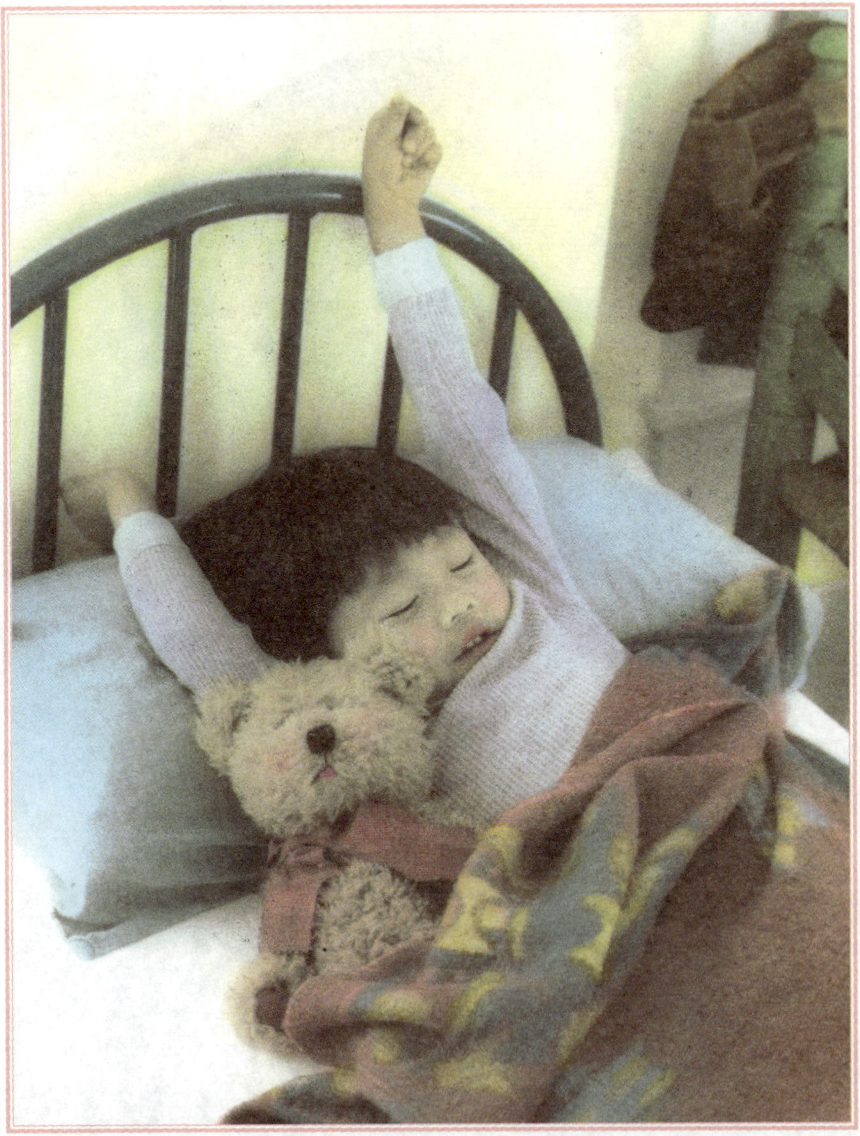

I have a busy day today, Jesus.
Help me to do my chores with cheer
and be kind to others,
even if they are not kind to me.
Watch over me as I walk the dog
and play with my friends.
Lord, I have a busy day.
Thank you for being by my side.
               Amen.

The First Day of School

When Robert saw the big school building and all the children, he whispered to his mother, "Do I have to go?"

"Yes, Robert," Mother said softly as she put her arms around him. "I know that you are nervous about your first day at school. Let's pray to Jesus to look out for you today." Mother and Robert prayed that he would not be lonely or scared at school. They walked through the school's big front door. When they reached his classroom, he heard a friendly voice.

"Hi, Robert," Scott called.

Robert's face broke into a smile when he saw his friend. "Are you in this class, too?" He wasn't afraid anymore. God sent him a friend.

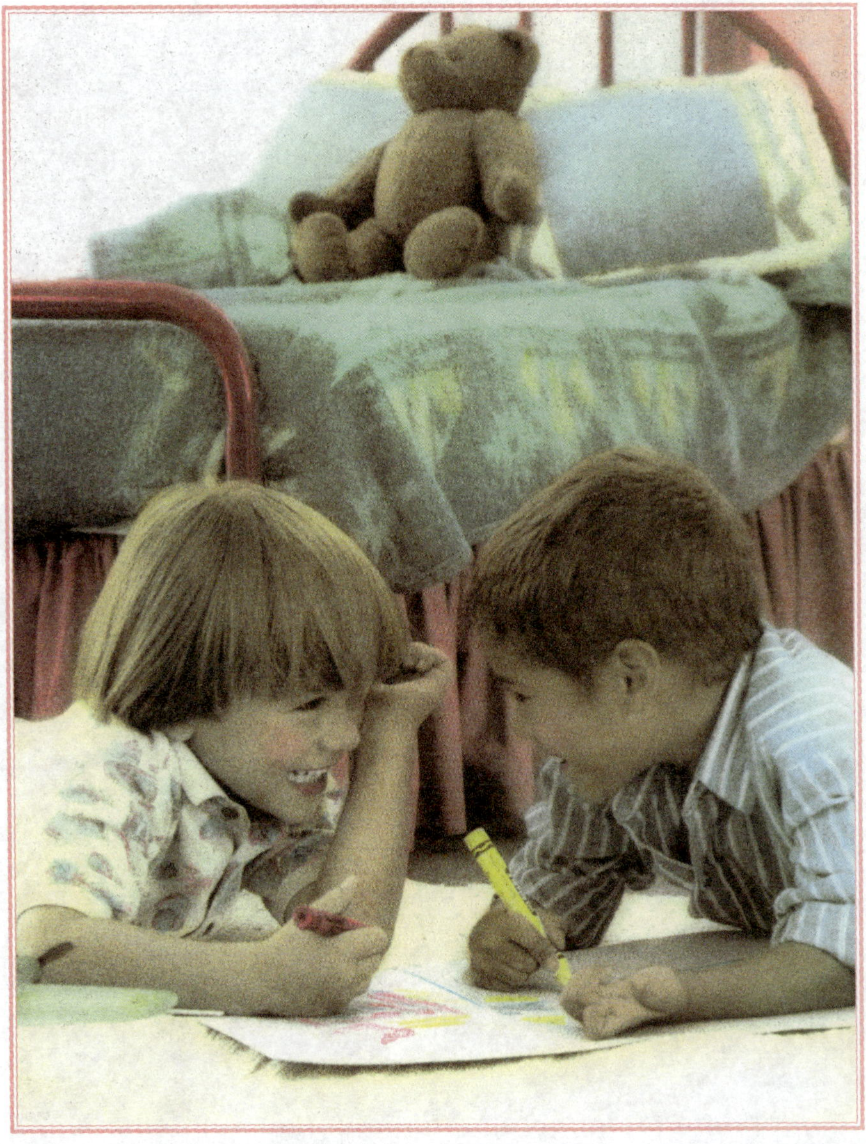

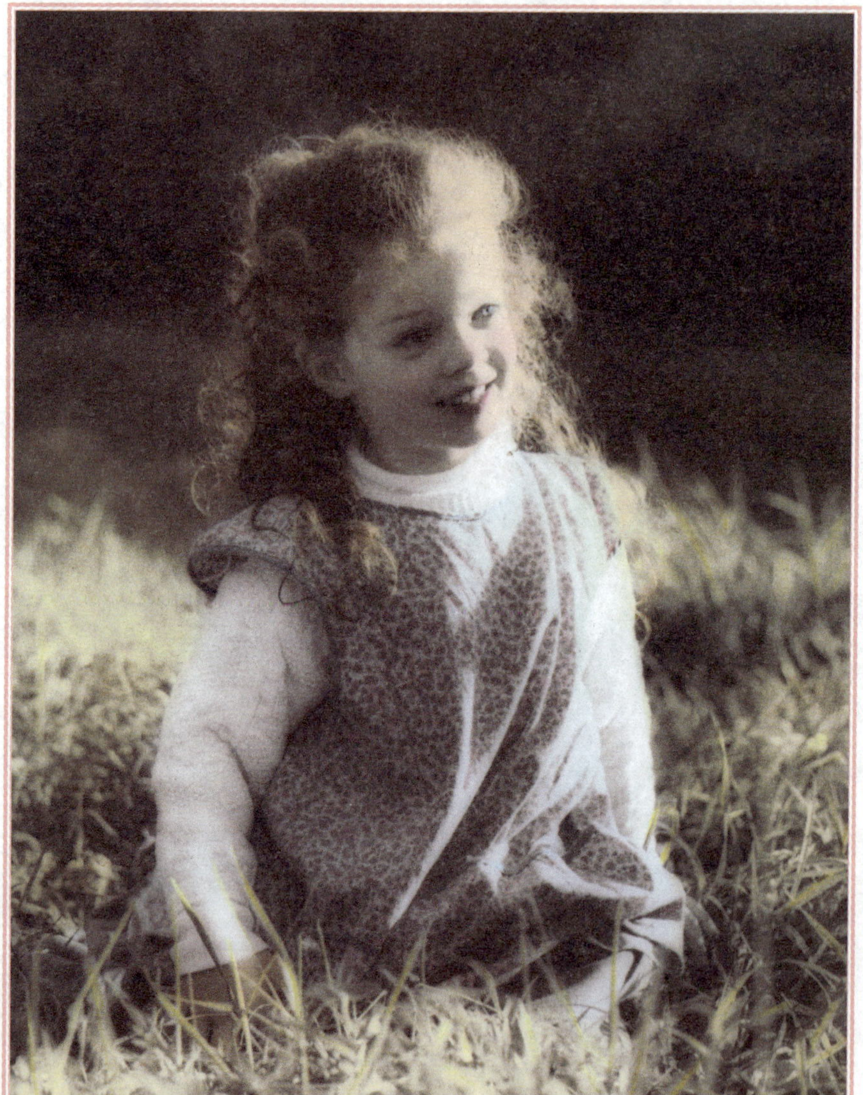

The year's at the spring
    And day's at the morn;
Morning's at seven;
    The hillside's dew-pearl'd;
The lark's on the wing;
    The snail's on the thorn;
God's in His heaven—
    All is right with the world.

Robert Browning

The Lord is all I need.
He takes care of me.

Psalm 16:5

For this new morning and its light,
    For rest and shelter of the night,
For health and food, for love and friends,
    For every gift Your goodness sends,
We thank You, gracious Lord.

This is the day which the Lord has made;
let us rejoice and be glad in it.

Psalm 118:24

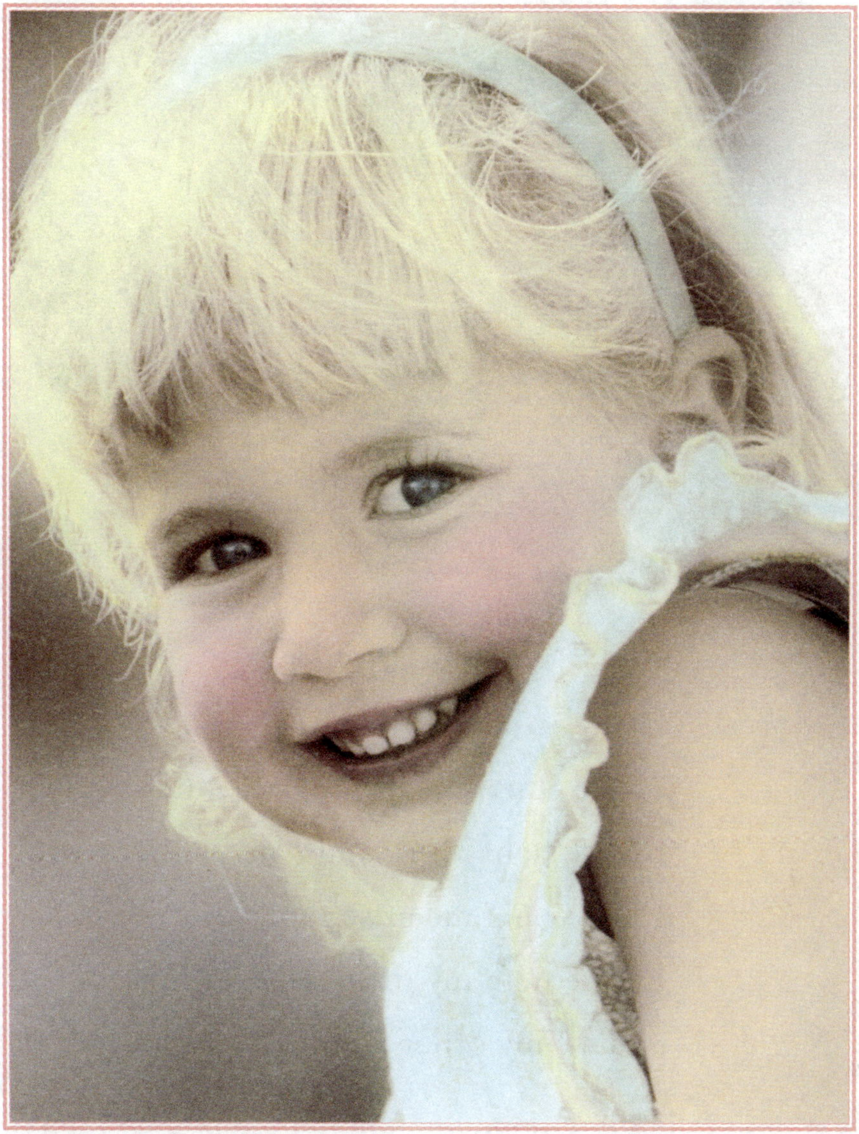

Dear Father,
As we start this day, please guide us.
Please help Mom and Dad as they work.
Please help me at school.
Please help my little sister at home,
and all my other friends and family.
                                    Amen.